T0025202

Seaside
Inspirations

Seaside
Inspirations

DISCOVER THE HEALING POWERS OF THE OCEAN

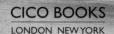

CICO BOOKS

LONDON NEW YORK

Published in 2023 by CICO Books

An imprint of Ryland Peters & Small Ltd

20–21 Jockey's Fields   341 E 116th St
London WC1R 4BW   New York, NY
                   10029

www.rylandpeters.com

10 9 8 7 6 5 4 3 2 1

Design and photography
© CICO Books 2023

A CIP catalog record for this book is
available from the Library of Congress
and the British Library.

ISBN: 978-1-80065-203-3

Printed in China

Compiled by: Kristine Pidkameny
Senior commissioning editor:
Carmel Edmonds
Editor: Slav Todorov
Designer: Paul Tilby
Art director: Sally Powell
Creative director: Leslie Harrington
Head of production: Patricia Harrington
Publishing manager: Penny Craig

"Your heart is the size of an ocean.

Go find yourself in its hidden depths."

RUMI

Introduction

Time spent at the seaside frees, heals, and inspires us. This beautiful compendium of words and stunning photography is your indispensable companion for a trip to the coast to ignite the senses and invite greater awareness, peace, and joy into your life. The gentle splashing of waves reaching the shore... the shimmering ripples across the ocean's surface as a breeze blows over it... the scent of fresh, salty air and the blue sky above... Water, and the elements associated with the seaside, can evoke an immediate sensory response in us. Nearly all of us are drawn to the tranquil allure of the deep ocean.

Within these pages discover the wonder and variety of seaside experiences. From the idyllic ease of the calm blue sea to the powerful messages of the wild when the ocean gets stormy, be transformed by nautical wisdom and joy. Connect with the poetry of the sea and its awe-inspiring views. In appreciating the beauty and romance of dreamy skies, sandy shores, and waterside settings you are changed for the better.

This captivating collection of seaside images and words is intended to inspire everyone. Whether you are on vacation, planning time away, or simply want to enjoy the lulling influence of the soft blue waves, welcome the abundant gifts of the sea.

"Still waters run deep."

ENGLISH PROVERB

CALM
SEAS

1

settle into
the tranquility
of now

blue opens
the way to
inner peace

"When I sit here by the sea and listen to the sound of waves, I feel free from all obligations and people of this world."

HENRY DAVID THOREAU

"Don't sit and wait.
Get out there, feel life.
Touch the sun, and
immerse in the sea."

RUMI

nourish your destiny

"We cannot see our reflection in running water. It is only in still waters that we can see."

ZEN SAYING

I connect with my true self

"Nothing is so strong as gentleness,

nothing so gentle as real strength."

SAINT FRANCIS DE SALES

"Now and then it's good to pause in our pursuit of happiness and just be happy."

GUILLAUME APOLLINAIRE

"Happiness is the settling of the soul
into its most appropriate spot."

ARISTOTLE

keep it simple

"Happiness not
in another place
but this place...
not for another
hour, but this hour."

WALT WHITMAN

breathe in
breathe out
get quiet

"The pursuit, even of
the best things, ought to
be calm and tranquil."

MARCUS TULLIUS CICERO

"Let the waters settle and you will see the moon and the stars mirrored in your own being."

RUMI

"My heart is tuned to the quietness that the stillness of nature inspires."

HAZRAT INAYAT KHAN

"A happy life consists in tranquility of mind."

MARCUS TULLIUS CICERO

"Calmness is the graceful
form of Confidence."

MARIE VON EBNER-ESCHENBACH

"Peace is always beautiful."

WALT WHITMAN

"Balance is the perfect state of still water. Let that be our model. It remains quiet within and is not disturbed on the surface."

CONFUCIUS

Memories
of the sea
lift my spirit
and soothe
my soul

my guiding
word
is serenity

"Returning to the source is serenity."

LAO TZU

"Tomorrow
is a new day.
You shall
begin it well
and serenely."

RALPH WALDO EMERSON

"Sometimes in the winds of change,
we find our true direction."

ANONYMOUS

2

BLUSTERY
SEAS

"Water is the driving force of all nature."

LEONARDO DA VINCI

"I'm not afraid of storms, for I'm learning how to sail my ship."

LOUISA MAY ALCOTT

"The real voyage of discovery consists not in seeking new landscapes, but in having new eyes."

MARCEL PROUST

> **“Above the clouds,
> the sky is always blue.”**
>
> THERESE OF LISIEUX

"Each day provides its own gifts."

MARCUS AURELIUS

"Roll on, thou deep
and dark blue ocean."

LORD BYRON

do everything today with intention

"Never give up, for that is just the

place and time the tide will turn."

HARRIET BEECHER STOWE

worrying will never change the outcome

"It is extraordinary to see the sea; what a spectacle!
She is so unfettered that one wonders whether it
is possible that she again become calm."

CLAUDE MONET

"I imagine therefore I belong and am free"

EMILY DICKINSON

let go

"But where, after all, would be the poetry of the sea were there no wild waves?"

JOSHUA SLOCUM

66 **The ocean is a mighty harmonist.** 99

WILLIAM WORDSWORTH

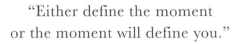

"Either define the moment
or the moment will define you."

WALT WHITMAN

"The heart of man is very much like the sea, it has its storms, it has its tides and in its depths it has its pearls too."

VINCENT VAN GOGH

3

NAUTICAL
WISDOM

life is
like the ocean
—an open
invitation

"Individually, we are one drop.
Together, we are an ocean."

RYUNOSUKE SATORO

"Nothing is softer or more flexible than water; yet nothing can resist it."

LAO TZU

"Open your eyes and see the

beauty that surrounds you."

ANONYMOUS

"Everything turns on your assumptions about it, and that's on you. You can pluck out the hasty judgment at will, and like steering a ship around the point, you will find calm seas, fair weather and a safe port."

MARCUS AURELIUS

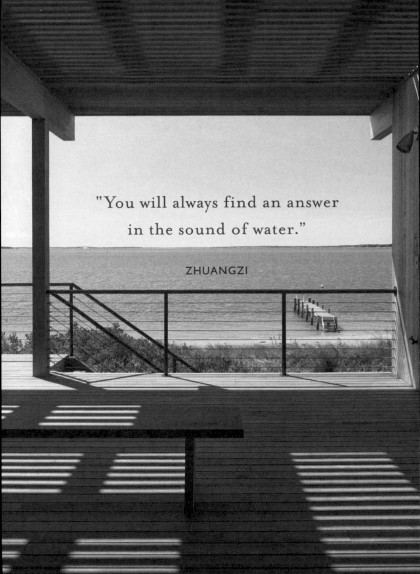

"You will always find an answer
in the sound of water."

ZHUANGZI

"Adopt the pace of nature."

RALPH WALDO EMERSON

life is happening right now

imagine flying into the blue

adventure
awaits

"Wonder is the beginning of wisdom."

SOCRATES

"Follow the river
and you will find the sea."

FRENCH PROVERB

connect with your divine source

awakened awareness is your true nature

honor the stillness

"To the mind that is still,
the whole universe surrenders."

LAO TZU

"A little sea-bathing
would set me up forever."

JANE AUSTEN

see the ocean...remain curious

water unites

"Knowledge born of the finest discrimination takes us to the farthest shore. It is intuitive, omniscient, and beyond all divisions of time and space."

PATANJALI

trust in the present moment

"I dwell in possibility."

EMILY DICKINSON

"Give every day the chance to become the most beautiful day of your life."

MARK TWAIN

"Never underestimate the healing effects of beauty."

FLORENCE NIGHTINGALE

"Truth lifts the heart,
like water refreshes thirst."

RUMI

SEA
ROMANCE

4

"The touch of the sea is sensuous, enfolding the body in its soft, close embrace."

KATE CHOPIN

"Drink deeply.

Live in serenity and joy."

BUDDHA

"What greater thing is there for two human souls than to feel that they are joined —to strengthen each other—to be at one with each other in silent unspeakable memories."

GEORGE ELIOT

"Wherever you go,

go with all your heart."

CONFUCIUS

"Some people look for a beautiful place, others make a place beautiful."

HAZRAT INAYAT KHAN

"Where waters do agree, it is quite wonderful the relief they give."

JANE AUSTEN

synchronize

with

nature

relax to the sound of
the gentle evening rain

"Music in the soul can be heard
by the universe."

LAO TZU

"My soul is full of longing for the secret of the sea, and the heart of the great ocean sends a thrilling pulse through me."

HENRY WADSWORTH LONGFELLOW

"The voice of the sea is seductive; never ceasing, whispering, clamoring, murmuring, inviting the soul to wander for a spell in abysses of solitude."

KATE CHOPIN

"Love one another,
but make not
a bond of love: Let it
rather be a moving sea
between the shores
of your souls."

KAHLIL GIBRAN

water sustains everything

"Oh the summer night,
has a smile of light,
And she sits on
a sapphire throne."

BRYAN PROCTER

blue is

a soft place

to land

be truthful,

gentle,

and fearless

"Be happy for this moment.
This moment is your life."

OMAR KHAYYAM

"There really is no better time than now."

SIR WALTER SCOTT

"Happiness depends upon ourselves."

ARISTOTLE

"Only from the heart
can you touch the sky."

RUMI

THE LOVE OF THE SEA, SAND, AND SKY

"I followed my heart
and it led me to the beach."

ANONYMOUS

"The sea
appears
all golden.
Beneath the
sun-lit sky."

HEINRICH HEINE

take time for you: imagine the possibilities

"I never get tired
of a blue sky."

VINCENT VAN GOGH

water expands our
horizons and nourishes
our perspective

"We dream
in colors
borrowed
from the sea"

UNKNOWN

marvel at the blue
of the sea and be happy

"The open Sky sits upon our senses like a Sapphire Crown —the Air is our robe of state— the Earth is our throne, and the Sea a mighty Minstrell playing before it..."

JOHN KEATS

"Blue color is
everlastingly appointed
by the deity to be
a source of delight."

JOHN RUSKIN

"THE SEA!

The sea! The open sea!

The blue, the fresh,

the ever free!"

BRYAN PROCTER

"If you should take the human heart and listen to it, it would be like listening to a sea-shell; you would hear in it the hollow murmur of the infinite ocean to which it belongs, from which it draws its profoundest inspiration, and for which it yearns."

EDWIN HUBBELL CHAPIN

the simple joys are the great ones

if you want to be happy be

"I will do water
—beautiful,
blue water."

CLAUDE MONET

"Live in the sunshine,
swim the sea,
drink the wild air."

RALPH WALDO EMERSON

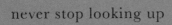

never stop looking up

downtime is your time

66 Forever
is composed
of nows. **99**

EMILY DICKINSON

"As for myself, the wonderful sea charmed me from the first."

JOSHUA SLOCUM

Credits

1 *ph.* Mark Lohman; 2 – 3 *ph.* Mark Lohman; 4 – 5 *ph.* Mark Lohman; 6 *ph.* Mark Scott; 8 – 9 *ph.* Earl Carter; 10 Crena Watson Photographer www.crenawatson.com/*ph.* Earl Carter; 11 *ph.* Jan Baldwin; 12 – 13 *ph.* Ian Wallace; 14 *ph.* Chris Tubbs; 15 *ph.* Caroline Arber; 16 *ph.* Paul Massey; 17 *ph.* Debi Treloar; 18 – 19 *ph.* Jan Baldwin; 20 *ph.* Earl Cater; 21 *ph.* Claire Richardson; 22 *ph.* Jan Baldwin; 23 *ph.* Mark Scott; 24 *ph.* Chris Tubbs; 25 *ph.* Mark Scott; 26 – 27 *ph.* Mark Scott; 28 *ph.* Paul Massey; 29 *ph.* Earl Carter; 30 *ph.* Earl Carter; 31 *ph.* Earl Carter; 34 *ph.* Mark Scott; 35 *ph.* Mark Scott; 36 Crena Watson Photographer www.crenawatson.com/*ph.* Earl Carter; 37 *ph.* Earl Carter; 38 – 39 *ph.* Paul Massey; 40 *ph.* Jan Baldwin; 41 *ph.* Earl Carter; 42 – 43 *ph.* Earl Carter; 44 *ph.* Jan Baldwin; 45 *ph.* Earl Carter; 46 *ph.* Peter Cassidy; 47 *ph.* Jan Baldwin; 48 – 49 *ph.* Paul Massey; 50 *ph.* Edina van der Wyck; 51 *ph.* Helen Cathcart; 52 – 53 The home of Rick Livingston and Jim Bawders, Quoge, New York/*ph.* Earl Carter; 54 *ph.* Francesca Yorke; 55 *ph.* Jan Baldwin; 56 – 57 *ph.* Peter Cassidy; 59 *ph.* Jan Baldwin; 60 – 61 *ph.* Paul Massey; 62 The home of Rick Livingston and Jim Bawders, Quoge, New York/*ph.* Earl Carter; 63 *ph.* Francesca Yorke; 64 *ph.* Jan Baldwin; 65 *ph.* Paul Massey; 66 – 67 *ph.* Ian Wallace; 68 The home of Cary Tamarkin & Mindy Goldberg on Shelter Island/*ph.* Earl Carter; 69 *ph.* Paul Massey; 70 *ph.* Pia Tryde; 71 *ph.* Georgia Glynn-Smith; 72 *ph.* Paul Massey; 73 The family home of Hanne Dalsgaard & Henrik Jeppesen in Zealand, Denmark/*ph.* Earl Carter; 74 – 75 *ph.* Paul Massey; 76 *ph.* Debi Treloar; 77 Crena Watson Photographer www.crenawatson.com/*ph.* Earl Carter; 78 *ph.* Ian Wallace; 79 *ph.* Jan Baldwin; 80 – 81 *ph.* Debi Treloar; 82 *ph.* Earl Carter; 83 *ph.* Georgia Glynn-Smith; 84 – 85 *ph.* Jan Baldwin; 87 *ph.* Jan Baldwin; 88 – 89 *ph.* Mark Scott; 90 *ph.* Paul Massey; 91 *ph.* Francesca Yorke; 92 – 93 *ph.* Mark Scott; 94 *ph.* Ian Wallace; 95 *ph.* Mark Scott; 96 – 97 The home in Denmark of Charlotte Lynggaard designer of Ole Lynggaard, Copenhagen/*ph.* Paul Massey; 98 *ph.* Paul Massey; 99 *ph.* Mark Scott; 100 – 101 *ph.* Mark Scott; 102 *ph.* Debi Treloar; 103 *ph.* Jan Baldwin; 104 Jan Constantine www.janconstantine. com/*ph.* Paul Massey; 105 *ph.* Jan Baldwin; 106 – 107 *ph.* Paul Massey; 108 *ph.* Earl Carter; 109 *ph.* Paul Massey; 110 – 111 *ph.* Earl Carter; 112 Stelle Architects; Dune House/*ph.* Paul Massey; 113 The home in Denmark of Charlotte Lynggaard designer of Ole Lynggaard, Copenhagen/*ph.* Paul Massey; 114 – 115 *ph.* Earl Carter; 116 *ph.* Mark Scott; 117 *ph.* Debi Treloar; 118 – 119 *ph.* Ian Wallace; 120 *ph.* Paul Massey; 121 *ph.* Debi Treloar; 122 Crena Watson Photographer www.crenawatson.com/*ph.* Earl Carter; 123 *ph.* Chris Tubbs 124 – 125 *ph.* Jan Baldwin; 126 *ph.* Jan Baldwin; 127 The home of Cary Tamarkin & Mindy Goldberg on Shelter Island/*ph.* Earl Carter; 128 – 129 *ph.* Debi Treloar; 130 *ph.* Jan Baldwin; 131 *ph.* Earl Carter; 132 – 133 *ph.* Earl Carter; 134 *ph.* Jan Baldwin; 135 *ph.* Jan Baldwin; 136 *ph.* Mark Scott; 137 *ph.* Paul Ryan; 138 *ph.* Christopher Drake; 139 *ph.* Chris Tubbs; 140 *ph.* Mark Scott; 141 *ph.* Jan Baldwin; 142 *ph.* Jan Baldwin; 143 *ph.* Georgia Glynn-Smith.